LOGISTICS

OF

FIFTH

DIMENSION

WAVES

Fi'D Waves

Also by Jerry D. C. Nelson

Logistics of Dreaming
www.iuniverse.com

A book that tells why and how we dream.
Discusses the three main types of dreams.
Shows the correct way to document dreams.

LOGISTICS
OF
FIFTH
DIMENSION
WAVES

The door to the Fifth Dimension is opened,
Accompanying is the Sixth & Seventh.

Second Edition

Jerry D.C. Nelson

iUniverse, Inc.
Bloomington

LOGISTICS OF FIFTH DIMENSION WAVES

iUniverse books may be ordered through booksellers or by contacting:

iUniverse
1663 Liberty Drive
Bloomington, IN 47403
www.iuniverse.com
1-800-Authors (1-800-288-4677)

Because of the dynamic nature of the Internet, any Web addresses or links contained in this book may have changed since publication and may no longer be valid. The views expressed in this work are solely those of the author and do not necessarily reflect the views of the publisher, and the publisher hereby disclaims any responsibility for them.

Any people depicted in stock imagery provided by Thinkstock are models, and such images are being used for illustrative purposes only.

Certain stock imagery © Thinkstock.

ISBN: 978-1-4401-0580-7 (sc)
ISBN: 978-1-4401-0581-4 (ebook)

Printed in the United States of America

iUniverse rev. date: 12/29/2010

This book is dedicated to my sweet and loving wife, Lucy.

Contents

PART III: SEQUEL DIMENSIONS

PART IV: FUNDAMENTAL FORCES

EPILOGUE

REFERENCES

Green, G. 2004 "THE FABRIC OF THE COSMOS" Vintage books: ISBN 0375-72720-5

Kaku, M. 2005 "PARALLEL WORLDS" Doubleday publishers:ISBN 0-385-50986-3

Magueijo, J. 2003 "FASTER THAN THE SPEED OF LIGHT" Penguin Books: ISBN 0-7382-0525-7

Witt, T. 2007 "OUR UNDISCOVERED UNIVERSE" Aridian Publishing Corporation ISBN -10: 0-9785931-3-8

BZ's 2007 San Francisco Fleetweek. US Navy aircraft http://home.comcast.net/~bz1a/

Encyclopedia Britannia Livescience http://www.livescience.com/technology

Wikipedia Free Encyclopedia www.nationmaster.com/encyclopia

PREFACE

When I was in high school, I was taught certain scientific "facts" that are no longer true. For instance, there were only 97 elements back than and an aircraft (propeller-driven) could not go faster than the speed of sound as the sound barrier would rip the plane apart. I also was taught that light is both a wave and a particle, nothing can travel faster than the speed of light and that light can travel in a vacuum, that is, light did not need a medium to travel on.

Where is this vacuum? The space beyond our atmosphere? The area between the Earth and the moon? The space between the moon and the sun? Those are only partial vacuums when you consider the gases, the electromagnetic waves and the particles thrown out by the sun, or the material spread out by passing comet tails. Also, there are the inter-planet magnetic and gravitational waves and scientists say that there could be many other dimensions sharing our space. Then there is antimatter, dark matter, dark energy and we have measured the Cosmic microwave back-ground radiation. To top all that off, Einstein has proposed the space fabric theory which relates to gravity and time in the fourth dimension. With all that stuff in space, there cannot be a true vacuum. So what is light, or electromagnetic waves, really traveling on in this so-called space? Are any of those mentioned items being used as a medium to carry electromagnetic waves?

All of those early lessons have bothered me most of my life because I have never found a satisfactory answer on how light is made, how light can be a wave and a particle at the same time and why does light travel at 299,792,458 m/s no matter the source or where the source is located: on Earth or in space. Because these questions bothered me, I started to investigate the mysteries of light and its waves. I then started to find some answers which led to more answers. To my surprise, I had an avalanche of discoveries all stemming from my assembly of "Laws of Waves." Now that I have answered the questions that had plagued me most of my life, I will share these discoveries.

PART ONE:

FOUNDATION

A WAVE IS

A WAVE IS

A WAVE

CHAPTER 1

SOUND WAVES

WAVE: An oscillation (rhythmic disturbance) moving from a point in a medium with time and can be described by mathematical specifications as to frequency, amplitude, phase and velocity.

To start my investigation, I began with something that I knew: sound waves. I wrote down all the parameters that I knew that control sound waves. My list started with six characteristics that I now label as Wave Laws. I thought that I had them all. Then every day I would discover another law that I had to incorporate in my list. This went on until there were 27 Wave Laws. Is this the end? I doubt it. I then divided the 27 laws into two sets: Primary and Secondary laws relating to their relative importance.

At this time, we will review the wave laws that have been assembled that govern sound waves. I am sure that you are already familiar with most of them as they are everyday common knowledge. It would behoove you to go over each of the 27 laws to make sure that you are thoroughly familiar with each law and how it relates to our world of sound. This will be of utmost importance when we apply them to electromagnetic waves. **Similarity** is the key.

Most of the wave laws are self-explanatory, but there are a few that may cause a little concern to a few people, therefore I will explain a few of the wave laws from the following list:

1

WAVE LAWS (for the birth, life, and death of a wave)

Primary:

1. All waves travel on or through a medium (i.e., a carrier) with little or no permanent displacement of the medium.
2. The wave consists solely of the medium.
3. The medium will have an essence/substance.
4. A wave can be either linear-directional or omni-directional.
5. The wave carries energy away from the wave source by the medium.
6. A wave will have a *Doppler effect* due to relative motion between the source and observer.
7. The dynamics/resonance of the medium determines the velocity the wave in that medium.
8. The terminal velocity of a wave is at the wave barrier.
9. A *shock wave* is formed at velocities greater than the wave barrier.
10. An object *cannot* pass through a shock wave as its generation is a continuous event.
11. A shock wave consists of noise (one or more random wave frequencies).
12. The shock wave is a noticeable attenuator (i.e., energy transformation).

Secondary:

13. A shock wave may distort the medium.
14. The velocity and shape of the object determines the energy transferred to the shock wave
15. A wave propagation is caused by another substance.
16. The dynamics of the medium and/or wave determine the attenuation of the wave.
17. The wave can be altered by another substance/object or a similar interacting wave.

18. The amplitude of energy carried by the wave. is determined by the wave source.

19. Whenever a parameter of the medium changes, the wave will change accordingly.

20. Gravity has no effect on a wave.

21. When two different frequency waves superimposed, they will heterodyne.

22. Wave amplitude can be increased through resonance in the medium.

23. Waves can be guided or reflected by a similar or dissimilar medium.

24. A waves energy can change media.

25. An object can transmit/receive one or more frequencies simultaneously.

26. Omni-directional waves can encircle obstacles, whereas linear directional waves cannot.

27. Noise frequencies will vary with the velocity of the projectile.

The list is split into two groups relating to their importance.The primary group defines what a wave is all about: the basic requirements. The secondary group relates more to the mechanical changes that vary with the medium or waves, which is common dynamics. Note that there are no "exceptions" stated in the Wave Laws.Our medium for sound waves is our breathable air, a gas (Law #1). Note that Law #2 states that the wave consists solely of the medium. Laws #2 and #3 are very important laws to remember for future reference. The terminal velocity of a sound wave in air is 770 mph (sea level @ 70 degrees F), which indicates the edge of the sound barrier (law #8). When an object passes the sound barrier, a shock wave will form (law #9).The shock wave is a great attenuator of the object's available energy (law #12). This velocity energy is transformed into wave frequency energy which forms the shock waves by friction. The shock wave will contain one or more frequencies. Lightning is a good example. The velocity of lightning is above the sound barrier, therefore a large shock wave develops. The shock wave carries all of its energy in the form of multiple frequencies: electrical and sound waves. All the audible frequencies for humans will be found in thunders which we consider as "noise." If close, you will just hear the "CRACK." If the lightning strike is in the distance, you may first hear some high frequency sounds, followed by the middle sounds then the low rumbling of the lower-frequency waves as it bounces around the country-side. The "CRACK" is the notification that the sound barrier has been breached. The most noticeable thing of the crack sound is that all the audible frequencies are in a small package for a short duration. Some of the noise from lightning also comes from the air being heated to high temperatures, causing a high rate of air expansion and contraction. The crack we hear from lightning contains sound frequencies up and beyond the upper limit of our hearing range, i.e., 20k cycles. The higher sound waves can be verified by our house pets. During an electrical storm, many pets are terrified by the high-intensity, high-frequency sounds. Dogs will howl and cats will hide under beds as they don't understand the significance of lightning. I even know people who are terrified of lightning. I'm not afraid of lightning, but I have the greatest respect for it, to where I'll give it a wide, wide berth.

The greater the velocity of an object moving in a medium above the wave barrier, the shorter the wavelength of the generated waves will be. A fixed number of wave cycles will have the same amount of energy no matter the time period in which they exist. That is, by compressing a fixed number of long waves into shorter waves, you will have a higher energy density. That is why the higher frequencies like gamma rays are more dangerous than longer waves. Wave Law #20 states that gravity has no effect on a wave. Gravity does have an effect on the medium's mass as a whole, not the individual molecular vibrations of its molecules. One can prove this by making a drawing of one long line of gas molecules then send a pulse down the line. No parameters of the gas molecules in that line will change other than the pulse movement of itself. Another way to say this, there is no change in the medium's mass due to the velocity of a wave in it. A wave does not change the weight/mass of its medium, therefore gravity does not see a wave. This would be a quiet world if all of the noise we generated was pulled to the ground by gravity. If you have closely followed the wave laws for sound, you should have no hesitation to use the wave laws in other areas. It is very important that you fully understand the first three laws and understand that they are inseparable for the rest of the wave laws. Note that "time" does not enter in any manner in the wave laws except in the concept of velocity.

Speed of Sound

There is a lot more information along with math on the characteristics of sound waves on the Internet. This is beyond the requirements of this book, but this information is available at Wikipedia free encyclopedia. You can go to its site:

www.nationmaster.com/encyclopedia/speed-of-sound

Shock Wave

Shock waves within the supersonic flow produce large gradients in air density and index of refraction by bending the light differentially on either side of the shock wave (Wave Law #13). A visual shock wave of this phenomenon may be seen with a low-flying U.S. Navy jet. See the 34th picture, dsc7901a, at:

http://home.comcast.net/~bzee1a/

Heat waves are more familiar to us. Wave Law # 13 states that a medium can be distorted. On a sunny day, at a distance, heat waves may be seen rising from a street pavement: this is distortion of the air medium. Anything that we see through and from beyond the heat waves will be seen distorted. This is the basis of mirages.

CHAPTER 2

AETHER

The Wave Laws should be applicable to all media, but it is questionable or difficult to apply them to non-ridged or soft materials to carry waves such as sand, rubber, lead or styrofoam. In fact, materials like these are used for sound deadening in many areas. One of the more interesting media in our daily lives would be H2O, or water, which has three phases. The wave characteristics will vary in each phase. Also, water has a surface wave that will be totally different from the sound waves carried through the water beneath the surface.

In the first chapter we were introduced to wave laws. All of them were recognized from my everyday experiences with sound, then recorded. I kept to the facts as best as I could; theories were not allowed. The intention was that these wave laws would explain the actions of all waves. The first chapter applied the wave laws to sound waves, which use the air we breathe as the medium. This should be easy for everyone to understand. Now the question is: will these wave laws developed from sound waves explain the actions of electromagnetic waves? We know that electromagnetic waves are true waves because we have manipulated them to where we fully understand all the octaves of the electromagnetic wave spectrum. These wave laws should apply equally to all electromagnetic waves, including light waves. But when we look at the wave laws, we are immediately faced with the big problem of law #2: the medium.

Yesteryear physicists surmised that light waves must travel through some particular medium, one that had never been seen or detected but must exist.

They gave this unseen light-caring stuff a name: the *luminiferous aether,* or *the aether* for short. When they measured the speed of light, it always came up the same regardless of their motion or that of the light's source. They could not explain this. Einstein knew that all experiments have failed to find *the aether*; therefore Einstein declared that "the speed of light is 670 million miles per hour relative to anything and everything." As "nothing can travel faster than light," let me state that this is a "manmade" law. Mother Nature's laws demand a medium for light waves.

X

The bottom line is that we not do know what the medium for electromagnetic waves is, but the wave laws require one. We can either state that it is *aether* or do what the mathematical world does when they come up with an unknown; they give it an unknown quantity of "X."

There is no reason that we cannot do the same by using the value of "X" to represent wave law # 1. Upon doing this, we now have answers for all the aspects of light waves. I have found that when I did not quite understand one of the wave laws as applied to light, I would review the wave as applied to sound waves, then apply the same action to light waves, I then would understand the law as applied to light. The wave laws do not show favoritism!

It is unreal that when we fill in the medium with an "X" for electromagnetic waves, we get many surprises as we look at the other laws. For instance: the speed of light does back up Einstein when he said that light travels the same velocity "relative to anything and everything," which really describes us as an inseparable part of the cosmos. We will understand this better when we compare this to sound waves. No matter how fast you travel when you make a noise, you cannot make sound waves go any faster or slower (at constant sea level). Thus we know that sound waves can move only at one constant speed, per law #7, and light waves have to follow the same law. The medium supports only one velocity for its waves without respect to other moving objects. From objects with relative motion to each other, we will get a difference in pitch, which we call the Doppler Effect. This is most noticeable when an emergency vehicle approaches us and then the pitch of the siren changes after it passes. Light waves experience the same Doppler Effect according to wave law # 6.

We also find that there is a light barrier just as there is for sound. This means that there is no velocity limit preventing matter from traveling faster than the speed of light! This is not an uncommon event in the cosmos; we just explain it off as some other phenomenon. What the wave law states is that there is a shock wave above the wave barrier. This is substantiated by the Cerenkov radiation, where the electron is traveling faster than the speed of light and gives off a blue light. This same principle can be applied in many other areas, which we will explain in a later chapter.

Now that we have an "X" for our medium, we have to find a "Y" and maybe a "Z" to mathematicaly solve for our unknown medium. We need to look into other areas to find them.

PART TWO:

PARALLEL WORLD

Dimensions are Visible by their
Disturbances

CHAPTER 3

FIFTH DIMENSION

When I started to work on the wave laws I knew that I lived in the third dimension because of the work of Einstein with the fourth dimension. He stated that the fabric of space-time was of the fourth dimension. My assumption was that we are floating in the fourth dimension because it surrounds us in the third dimension. That is, the fourth-dimension substance broke through the fabric of space into our third dimension as the result of the Big Bang. Because Einstein had claimed the fourth dimension for his fabric of space and time theory, I had to give ground and look for another medium for light to travel on. I then figured that there is no reason why the fourth and fifth dimensions couldn't have warped through that space hole at the same time. So I was forced to go with the fifth dimension supplying the medium for electromagnetic waves.

I had no proof if there was such a thing as a fifth dimension. Then I read Michio Kaku's book PARALLEL WORLDS, where on page 219 was Einstein's question: "And where is the fifth dimension?" Kaku said: "The answer is: we are floating in the fifth dimension, but we cannot enter it……...." Wonderful, he backed me up --- or, I backed him up! Michio Kaku has the name and the math, while I have the *wave laws*. Everything fell into place.

What startling information for me. I now had the needed proof that there is a fifth dimension. When I plugged the fifth dimension into the #1 wave law as the medium, all the parameters of electromagnetic waves fell into place. It was very exciting. In fact, even today, it is very hard for me to believe all

13

the discoveries that fifth dimension has led to. I owe a lot to Mr. Kaku for my use of his fifth dimension work. On the other hand, he used Einstein's fourth dimension in relating to Maxwell's work. Look at all the dimensions that have been freed and can now fly around. This is just the beginning of an exciting time.

Y

Rephrasing what Kaku said is that: "some stuff from the fifth dimension came into our 3rd dimension (during the Big Bang) which now carries our electromagnetic waves." This is our "Y" stuff or "Y" medium. I have given this "stuff" (or particles) its own name: **FIMENIUM**, from the words **Fi**fth **Dimen**sion Med**ium**.. Pronounced: Fi-men-ium. Trade-marked names use up the more choice names.

When you put in fimenium as the medium in the wave laws, then all aspects of light waves have true scientific answers, that is, all 27 wave laws will have solid understandings, especially when you compare them to sound waves. There is nothing wrong with going back to sound waves to see how a specific law works as I have done many times. To me, fimenium is the correct medium to put in for law #1 because all the other 26 wave laws fall into place. How can 26 wave laws be wrong?

I cannot overstress the importance of *wave laws* #1 and #2. For a wave to travel, it has to have a medium to travel on. Still, you cannot weigh light any more than you can weigh my voice traveling through the air. You cannot weigh waves, as they are just oscillations of the substance in the medium. Does a medium have to have a substance in order to carry radio waves? How else can you *exchange energy* from one medium to another? This validates wave law #3.

You breathe CO_2 in and out every minute of the day. You can't see it, smell it, taste it or touch it, yet you know that it carries your sound waves and it is all around you: "you are floating in CO_2....." and have no daily use for it. In comparison, you know that we live in the third dimension and you have heard that there are several other dimensions around us. So, it should be of no surprise to you when Kaku said: "we are floating in the fifth dimension........." How can that be? I can't see it, feel it, smell it, or touch it and I have absolutely no use for it, and now, Kaku has the nerve to state that it carries our light waves!

We have just learned that there is a fifth dimension and it is all around us. It permeates every fraction of everything in and around us, the universe and the cosmos. You cannot see it or touch it but you can prove that it is there by mathematics and by the fact that it carries light. Therefore, fimenium has to have substance and eventually we will be able to detect and measure fimenium, When we do, we will be able to calculate the mass of fimenium which means that we have found the elusive *Dark Matter.*

We have "X" as stipulated my Mother Nature. And now we have fimenium or "Y" as a math validation for "X." What we need now is something to validate "Y." that is, a substantial "Z."

CHAPTER 4
ELECTROMAGNETIC WAVES

Upon analyzing his equations, Maxwell found that changes or disturbances to electromagnetic fields travel in a wavelike manner at a particular speed: 670 million miles per hour. As this is precisely the same value other experimenters had found for the speed of light, Maxwell realized that light must be nothing other than an electromagnetic wave, one that has the right properties to interact with our eyes. Maxwell attempted to explain the speed his equations gave in the following way: "water waves or sound waves are carried by a substance, a medium, and the speeds of these waves are specified with the respect to the medium."

I found the book by Michio Kaku very interesting and informative. In fact, all my discoveries involving electromagnetic waves had evolved from what I have learned in that book. My main enlightenment came on page 199 where Kaku wrote: "In other words, Maxwell's theory of the electromagnetic force tumbles right out of Einstein's equations for gravity if we simply add a fifth dimension. Although we cannot see the fifth dimension, ripples can form on the fifth dimension, which correspond to light waves!"

Z

We have found a value for "Y," or fimenium, which is a bona fide medium for light waves. We know that light waves are just a band of waves in the electromagnetic spectrum that our eyes are tuned to. Now we will turn our attention to the electromagnetic waves as a whole, which will be our "Z" solution to our math problem. We will review how electromagnetic (EM) waves are made in our third dimension. We create EM waves when we flow AC or DC current down a wire (a conductor). Electrons flowing down a wire will create a magnetic field and a radio wave: thus its name "electromagnetic wave," Basically, as electrons flow down a wire, they are actually trying to pass through the fifth dimension medium (fimenium), but instead, are pushing fimenium aside. This will undoubtedly surprise many that we have something floating in a solid material. It will be substantiated later that fimenium is infinitesimally smaller than an electron or proton, therefore fimenium permeates all matter as if it was not there. Fimenium does not see solid obstacles. Also, we will find out that fimenium is a negative substance, therefore, electrons and fimenium are not compatible.

The fimenium that is being pushed outside of the wire by AC current is forming a field. This field is generating a frontal wave (our "Z") which is propagating through space. This is similar to a boat moving through water and making a bow wave. Note the displacement of water from under the boat which corresponds to our displacement of fimenium from the wire. The field is maintained as long there is current.

Now look at the wire as in a transformer or an antenna. When we pass current down a wire, the leading electrons will generate a magnetic field which in turn will create an electromagnetic wave (our "Z") in the medium, which spreads out from the wire to the surrounding space (fimenium). When that traveling wave crosses another wire, being negative, it will displace/push negative electrons down that wire similar to the wind pushing on the sails of a sailboat. For that same reason, when the current stops in our originating wire, the magnetic field around that wire collapses back into the wire, thus pushing the electrons in that wire as if they had sails, thus Back EMF.

To review what was just said, it is important to note that electrons and fimenium are not compatible as they are both negative entities. One can see that passing electrons through a conductor will push fimenium aside, which is identical for passing fimenium waves that will push electrons aside in a conductor. Now we understand how electrons moving down a wire will transmit waves into space, and those waves will move electrons in the next wire, thus transmitting energy from one conductor to another. This is what makes radio transmitters, receivers and transformers possible.

The electrons moving down a wire will cause a frontal wave which is our "Z wave" being transmitted through space. Wave Law number 2 states that: " a wave consists solely of the medium." In this case, that medium is fimenium. Our "Z wave" is verification for "Y" and for what Kaku said: "we are floating in the fifth dimension (fimenium)."

Wave Attenuation

Wave Law number 16 states that: "The dynamics of the medium and/or wave determines the attenuation of the wave." This means that our medium for light waves has to have an attenuation factor. If we find that factor, we have further proof of Wave Law number 2, that waves need a medium. It turns out that we have physical proof that a light wave does attenuate over a distance and it has been called: tired light, ancient light and lumetic decay.

This was not fully understood in the past. In fact, it was thought that the decay in the wave color was due to an expanding universe, but now it is known that light has to have a carrier, and the carrier will have a dynamic resistance which explains all the terminology used for weakening light waves.

In the book "OUR UNDISCOVERED UNIVERSE" by Terence Witt, page 261, he states: "Photon with twice its original wave length and half its original energy.......represents a distance on the order of 10Gly (ten billion light years)". This clearly shows that a light wave has a fixed speed, but it has to give up frequency as it gets weaker, which we detect as a lower shift in color.

Fimenium Wave

What we presently call an "electromagnetic wave" is not so; there is nothing electric or magnetic about it. That radio wave is just an ordinary wave moving in a medium: fimenium. Even though "radio wave or light wave" is still correct terminology, it does not encompass all waves, particularly the higher frequency waves such as gamma rays or X-rays. The term fifth-dimensional wave, or fimenium wave, would be more correct, as it would encompass all waves being carried through space.

Wave Drawings

The next pages are a pictorial view of the movement of electrons.

Drawing 4.1 shows three different types of waves and how they affect us. Drawing 4.2 shows electrons moving down a wire causing a magnetic field and a shock wave. The shock wave travels through space until it crosses another conductor, which will cause electrons to flow due to the incompatibility of waves and electrons.

CHAPTER 4

SYNOPSIS OF WAVES

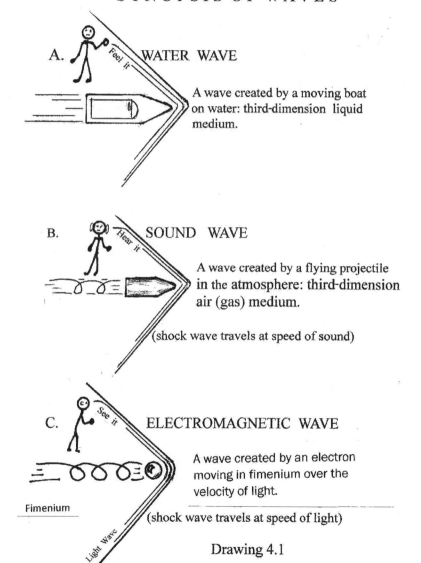

A. WATER WAVE

A wave created by a moving boat on water: third-dimension liquid medium.

B. SOUND WAVE

A wave created by a flying projectile in the atmosphere: third-dimension air (gas) medium.

(shock wave travels at speed of sound)

C. ELECTROMAGNETIC WAVE

A wave created by an electron moving in fimenium over the velocity of light.

Fimenium

(shock wave travels at speed of light)

Drawing 4.1

21

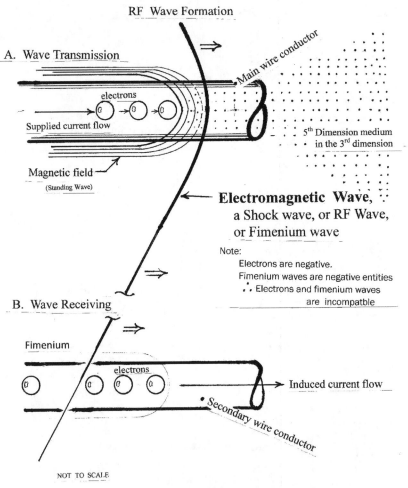

RF Wave Formation

A. Wave Transmission

electrons

Supplied current flow

Main wire conductor

Magnetic field
(Standing Wave)

5th Dimension medium
in the 3rd dimension

Electromagnetic Wave,
a Shock wave, or RF Wave,
or Fimenium wave

Note:
Electrons are negative.
Fimenium waves are negative entities
∴ Electrons and fimenium waves
are incompatble

B. Wave Receiving

Fimenium

electrons

Induced current flow

Secondary wire conductor

NOT TO SCALE

Drawing 4.2

CHAPTER 5

VALIDATION

Chapter 1 presented the Wave Laws which dictate the need of a wave carrier for all waves. Then in chapter 3 we found that light waves, because they are waves, have a medium we now call fimenium. We have the math which names the carrier and we have the visual proof of the carrier when it carries light waves: making it possible for you to read this book and see the world around you.

What we are missing is the actual physical proof of fimenium and what fimenium is composed of molecularly. We will now look for the physical proof to validate fimenium .

Magnetism

You should have noticed by now that the magnetic field is a by-product of current flowing in a conductor, thus through fimenium. We know that electrons repel fimenium because they both are negative in nature. We know that protons are positive so they should attract fimenium. And they do. This is why we get a build-up of fimenium around the wire that does not get too far away from the conductor. Protons will not allow the displaced fimenium to dissipate into space, which gives the fimenium field the necessary momentum to move back into the conductor when the current stops, resulting in a Back EMF.

We know that the electrons move in one direction, which means the positive fields of the protons are moving in the opposite direction. When the electron is moving from one atom to the next atom, the atom it left becomes positive, and the atom the electron is moving to will lose its positive potential. So the positive fields will seem to be moving in the opposite direction of the current flow. This gives us the expression "current flows in one direction while electricity flows in the opposite direction."

You can see that we have the flowing electrons pushing fimenium out of the conductor, while the protons are struggling to retain the fimenium. We have two strong forces acting in the opposite directions, which is compressing fimenium into another phase that we call a "magnetic field."

We have a phase change in the third dimension, which we are very familiar with. When we compress CO_2 in a cylinder and piston, then remove the generated heat, we get what we call "Dry Ice," which is a phase change. We recognize that it is the same CO_2 in the two different phases: as a gas we cannot see or touch it, while as a solid state we can see and "**feel**" it.

Fimenium has a similar phase change. As a fifth-dimensional gas, it carries all our fimenium waves. After being compressed into a fifth-dimensional fluid between protons and electrons, it attains an affinity for iron. This "fifth-dimensional fluid," which we call a "magnetic field," produces a force that we can "**feel**" when it comes in the vicinity of iron. This physical reaction of the force field, or magnetic field, is our physical proof of fimenium (fifth-dimension medium).

We can show the similarity between the two phases of fimenium. When a wave is transmitted across space and it engages a conductor, the wave will cause a current to flow because of the repulsion forces between the negative wave and negative electrons. Now, take a magnet and move it across that same conductor, what do you get? The negative field of the magnet will cause negative electrons to flow in the conductor. Is there a difference between the field of the magnet and the fimenium wave as they cross a conductor?

Note that it takes the action of both electrons and protons to create a magnetic field. The action of flowing electrons alone will not cause a magnetic field, which is the case of flowing electrons inside a vacuum tube. There are no magnetic fields formed between the anode and cathode in a tube. Also, there are no magnetic fields around a spark in a vacuum.

CHAPTER 6

SPECULATION

So far, the material in this book has been pretty much straight-forward as we have only been observing Mother Nature to understand how the world of physics around us works when applied to waves. All that I have been doing is describing how nature's wave laws work, with the exception of coining a new word, fimenium, to describe one of nature's materials/media.

Now, I hit a muddy road with large pot-holes that could swallow one up. It is necessary for us to go over our road map to find out where we are.

We have found that:

X = a medium that carries waves (including electromagnetic waves).

Y = a medium that carries light waves (an electromagnetic wave) = fimenium

Z = a medium that carries all electromagnetic waves

We have X = Y = Z = fimenium.

What is fimenium?

Fimenium

This is what we know about fimenium:

1. It is "stuff" from another dimension.

   We know this because we have a math theory
   that so states.
   We know this because it has a field.

2. It has a negative field.

   We know this because it is incompatible with
   electrons, which are negative.
   It has an attraction to the protons, which are
   positive.

3. It has two phases as compared to third-dimension phases.

   We know this because we are surrounded by the gas
   phase (primary phase), which carries light.
   And the liquid phase (secondary phase) forms
   around a wire, what we call magnetism.

4. The particles that make up fimenium's substance has to be very
   small as compared to electrons.

   It would be like comparing sand to a soccer ball or
   air molecules to a golf ball.
   That is: fimenium particles are $1/2000^{th}$ to $1/5000^{th}$ the
   size of an electron.
   We know this because fimenium penetrates everything
   everywhere. There is absolutely "no place"
   without fimenium; from the center of the earth
   to the ends of the cosmos.
   We know this because we receive light waves from every
   place/direction in the cosmos.
   We know that magnetism will easily pass through all non-
   metallic materials, even some metals. To do this,
   the particles of fimenium have to be smaller than the
   components in a molecule in order for waves to

pass freely through the materials without interference.

We know that waves such as X-rays and gamma rays can penetrate most materials. We know that all waves need a medium to carry them and this means that any material that those waves pass through, has to have fimenium though out that material. Again, the particles of fimenium have to be smaller than the electrons or protons which make up all those molecules in order to carry X-rays and Gamma rays through any matter.

Now, which particle did I just describe?

We have a lot of theories on unknown particles in the micro-world like bosnons, Leptons, Hadrons, Tachyons, Tazons, Quarks, Mesons and Neutrinos, all of which we may not fully understand. This is a partial list, as I know that there are other particles out there waiting to be discovered: one could be for fimenium.

Neutrino

The best candidate I have found from the previous list is the neutrino. We know the neutrino is very small, it is believed that it can go through the entire Earth without hitting a thing. There are several organizations looking to prove the existence of the neutrino. The main problem is that they are looking for a neutral or positive neutrino and our neutrino has a negative field or a negative flavor.

Because our negative neutrino is so small, and we are surrounded by them, there can be no space in the cosmos free of them. Compare that to being on the bottom of the ocean: how would you use a water pump to make a space free of water to measure the weight of water? How would you manipulate a molecule of water? How can we manipulate a particle of fimenium to test it when we are immersed in it and it permeates everything.?

CHAPTER 7

MAGNETS

This chapter will show how permanent magnets develop and hold magnetic fields. To start, we will review the electromagnet field as covered in chapter 4. A flow of electrons in a wire conductor will cause fimenium to propagate outwards from the conductor, thus starting a field. This field is due to the negative electron evacuating the negative fimenium from the wire. The electrons cannot leave the wire, but fimenium can. That magnetic field will be stationary around the conductor as long as there is a steady flow of electrons.

Then there was the question: if the electrons are pushing the fimenium field out from the conductor, why doesn't the field just dissipate outwards from the conductor, like the displaced water from a boat bow? We have the negative force of the electron pushing the fimenium outwards, and the positive force of the proton attracting the fimenium, thus fimenium is compressed into another phase: magnetism.

E.M. Waves

We have just reviewed why there is a magnetic field around a wire conductor when current is flowing, and from present knowledge, we know that this is the same magnetic field around a permanent magnet. We know this to be true because in the case of a generator or electric motor, the stator can be either a permanent magnet or it can be an electromagnet; the output power can be identical in either case.

Therefore, the magnetic field around the permanent magnet is the same magnetic field around a conductor carrying current: an electro-magnet. That magnetic field is actually the fifth-dimension medium in a phase change in all cases.

Magnets

Drawing 7.1 shows an electro-magnet with the directions of current and the magnetic fields. The electro-magnet has a soft iron core where the inner domains of the molecules can align with the fields of the conductors, but cannot hold their alignment when the current ceases. Note that the iron core produces a larger magnetic field because of the numerous small fields of the wires being added together.

It is no secret that with the proper hard ferromagnetic materials, the domains of the molecules will stay aligned after the inducing magnetic field has been removed from the ferromagnetic material. The question is: how can the magnetic field maintain itself when there is no current flowing in the magnet? Don't forget, fimenium permeates everything, even the molecules in the magnetic material. Which means that the electrons are tunneling through the fimenium while in their orbit around the nucleus and causing molecular standing waves. Again, the electrons are pushing aside fimenium as it rotates around the nucleus and the protons in the nucleus are still attracting the fimenium from escaping; this is shown in drawing 7.2, view a -- a. We have the same event going on in the atomic world that we do in our world of a wire carrying a current. It is the unusual ability of iron to realign its domains that makes it so useful as a magnet.

We should understand now that when we are handling a permanent magnet, we are holding a condensed part of the fifth dimension. You cannot see it, weigh it, or feel it, but you know it is there by the reaction you can get with the magnet on other iron materials. Notice how the magnetic field can pass through your hands; that is exactly what fimenium has the ability to do because its particles are so infinitesimal. The field, fimenium, coexists with us like a parallel world and we are not aware of it: we are floating in it. This is why light has the same velocity no matter where the source is, because fimenium permeates everything in the cosmos. I have noticed that gravity does not have the attraction for fimenium that protons do.

CHAPTER 7

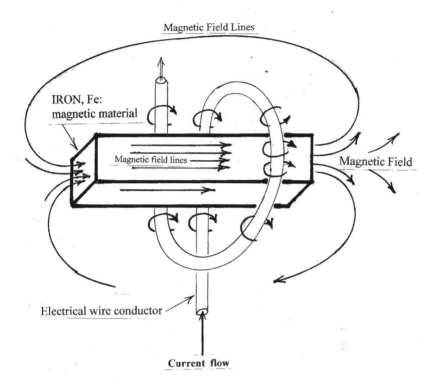

Magnetic Field Lines

IRON, Fe:
magnetic material

Magnetic field lines

Magnetic Field

Electrical wire conductor

Current flow

ELECTRO-MAGNET

NOT TO SCALE

Drawing 7.1

31

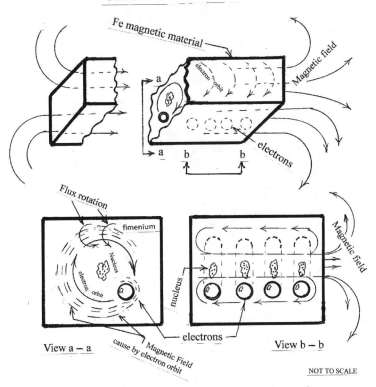

PERMANENT MAGNETS

View a—a is showing one electron rotating in its orbit around the nucleus. Note the electron is creating a magnetic field identically as it would if traveling down a wire expelling fimenium in its path.

View b – b shows four rotating electrons representing four molecules. Note the alignment of flux lines between molecules through the whole Fe bar. This is due to the ability of the iron to rotate its inner shells in alignment with other molecules.

Drawing 7.2

PART THREE:

SEQUEL DIMENSIONS

3rd DIMENSION
Can Manipulate The

6th DIMENSION
To Manipulate The

5th DIMENSION

CHAPTER 8
STATIC FIELDS

This chapter started out to be about STATIC ELECTRICITY, but, I found that it is so intertwined with the STRING THEORY that I will have to discuss both at this time.

The String Theory is thoroughly explained in many available sources, especially in PARALLEL WORLDS (by M. Kaku), therefore, I will not try to add anything to it. On page 190 in PARALLEL WORLDS is stated that all subatomic particles appear to be spinning like a miniature top.

Then on page 204 it states that the electron has a half-integral spin and is called a fermion and has negative charge. From a simple experiment we can develop an electrical static field around an excess of electrons (negative charge) or shortage of electrons (positive charge) and we can show that like charges repel each other while opposite charges attract each other. From that information, we can deduce that the proton has an opposite spin and has a positive charge.

Therefore, I can safely say that the electron and proton are energetic vibrating strings with a spin on them and because of their energetic status they should be causing a disturbance in their medium. A localized disturbance from another medium will show up in the third dimension as a field. We know that the magnetic field is a disturbance of the medium of the fifth dimension in the third dimension. Now, we have another disturbance of a medium, the static field, in the third dimension.

I find no similarity between the static field and the magnetic field. This can lead to only one conclusion; we are looking at two different media, that is, two different parallel worlds. We are now looking for another dimension(s), which is covered in the next chapter.

CHAPTER 9
OTHER DIMENSIONS

We have investigated the fifth dimension and proved that it exists by math and its' ability to carry light waves. According to Wave Law # 3, fimenium has to have substance in order for wave energy to traverse on it to full fill Wave Laws #1 and # 2. Because fimenium can be disturbed by moving electrons, we know that the particles of fimenium have a negative field. We can detect this field in the third dimension as an energy field which we have labeled: a *magnetic field*. Even though we can not dissect an energy field or presently test for its mass (weight), we know that it is present by other tests and observations. Thus, because of this negative energy field that fimenium has, I feel that this is sufficient proof that if any particle has its own energy field, then that particle has come from another dimension, a dimension existing in parallel (intra-existence) with our third dimension.

String Theory

When we put the *String Theory* into any equation we have a whole new picture of action and reaction. We suspect that the *Strings* contain very energetic waves which could give it substance. Also, particular variations of vibrations will give us different particles and these particles have a form of rotation which gives us the needed positive and negative relationship in the third dimension. Lastly, the vibrating strings/waves of energy should be the driving force in its medium, which the third dimension detects as an energy field, such as the negative field of the fimenium particle.

> *"In comparison to this bizarre-sounding claim, the difficulty in making a detailed alignment between string vibrational patterns and known particle species seems like a secondary issue. Superstring theory requires the existence of six dimensions of space that no one has ever seen. That's not a fine point --that's a problem": page 359 in*

THE FABRIC OF THE COSMOS, by Brian Greene.

Like the disturbance of the fifth dimension in the third dimension (the negative field), this should be also true for the sixth dimension. That is, if the sixth dimension has energetic superstrings, we should be able to detect its disturbances in the third dimension as an energy field. It so happens that we have an energy field that fits the description: the electrical static field!

Sixth Dimension

Electrons have a negative static field that we cannot dissect, thus making it an energy field from another dimension. We know that electrons have a negative electrical charge and the protons have a positive electrical charge and they both independently have a static field or charge. This indicates that both the electron and proton are vibrating superstrings of another dimension(s). We know from experiments that the electron has a CCW rotation (a negative spin) while the proton has a CW spin, thus the mutual attraction. The vibrating superstrings could be vibrating around their own centers, but due to possible difference in configurations, they are seen as a rotating particle in the third dimension. Note: the rotation of the electron is critical in the forming of linear light waves.

At first, I believed that both the electron and proton came from the same dimension, the energy dimension, sixth dimension. They are both similar as they both have a static field. Other than that, they are quite different. Some of the differences between the electron and proton are: their polarities, their physical size, their reactions to the fifth dimension and their energies. From what I have observed of previous "dimensions" they are mostly "singularities."

For this reason, I have put the electron and proton in their own individual dimensions.

The electron is the particle that carries most of the energy in the third dimension. When you heat up or cool down a particle of matter, it will be the electrons in the molecule that will increase or decrease their velocity. It is the movement of the electrons in orbit that determines the thermo energy of the molecule. It is the movement of electrons that forms sparks and lightning. Because the electron displays all of the energy in the molecule, it has to be from the energy dimension, which is the sixth dimension.

Seventh Dimension

Because we have put the electron in the sixth dimension, and we know that the proton has a positive energy field, it has to be from another dimension too. Because I have no math to prove what dimension the proton came from, this means that the proton will have the next dimension, the seventh dimension.

I would like to know more about the energy that vibrates those strings as wave forms. We theorize that those strings are highly energetic, giving us a very important *field* for the existence of all molecules. To keep the strings in vibrating and creating fields requires unlimited energy. How does the sixth and seventh dimension develop this energy? I feel that the sixth dimension supplies the *Dark Energy* to the cosmos being carried by fimenium waves.

CHAPTER 10
PARALLEL WORLDS

"Of course, the lack of observational evidence for extra dimensions might also mean they don't exist and that superstring theory is wrong. However, drawing that conclusion would be extremely hasty": THE FABRIC OF THE COSMOS by Brian Greene, page 18.

We talk about parallel worlds and many books have been written on the subject like "PARALLEL WORLDS" by Michio Kaku, but no one has come up with solid physical evidence that there are parallel worlds or other dimensions.

That is, until now. I believe that I have proved that the fifth dimension is all around us, that we are floating in it. The mathematical proof is from Theodr Kaluza's calculations along with Einstein's equations for gravity (PARALLEL WORLDS, page 199). When you plug in the fifth dimension into those two equations, you get ripples, which we perceive as light. Now, when you plug in the fifth dimension as the medium into the Wave Laws, you will find that all the parameters for light (or electromagnetic waves) are answered; this is our mechanical proof. For physical proof, just play around with a magnet and pass the unseen field through any solid object. That field is the fifth dimension, which shows that two dimensions can occupy the same space at the same time.

For an experiment for children, put a magnet under a glass table (or cardboard) and put a nail on top of the glass, over the magnet. Now move the magnet around and you will see the nail follow. That magnetic field is passing through the glass as if the glass weren't there. The glass and magnetic field are occupying the same space at the same time. That is how other dimensions can be around us and we do not know it.

We should be able to test all other *fields* the same way. We have tested the magnetic field, electrical static field, and the gravitational field. I have found that the magnetic field is in the fifth dimension and I have put the negative static field, along with the energy field, in the sixth dimension. The positive static field seems to be of the seventh dimension. Einstein has put time and gravitation in the fourth dimension and we are in the third dimension. Then Mr. Brian Greene in his book "THE FABARIC OF THE COSMOS," on page 18 states ".....a cosmic substrate composed of a total of eleven space-time dimensions." This means that we have eleven dimensions, or, Parallel Worlds occupying the same space that we are standing or sitting in right now. Do you feel crowded?

CHAPTER 11
ELEVENTH DIMENSION

How did life begin on this planet? Did a meteor carry the first single-cell organism here? Did a lightning bolt hit a pool of minerals that aligned the minerals into a cell? Did a windstorm cause a pool of chemicals to mix itself up into a life cocktail? I suppose it is all possible, but I find it very hard to believe.

Now that we know that there are eleven parallel worlds, how do they interface with life in the third dimension? So I tried to get an insight on the other dimensions. First I looked at the fourth dimension: gravity. I see no connection to life possibilities there. Then it was the fifth dimension: magnetism. I see no connection to the beginning of life there either. Next it was the sixth and the seventh dimension: electrons, protons and static electricity. We do need all of those items to build atoms. Still, that doesn't guarantee that they will all come together automatically in the right amounts to form a living cell. So, what do we really need to start life on this planet? We need **a catalyst!** A catalyst that promotes chemical reactions to form complex molecules, proteins and DNA strings.

We have seen how other parallel dimensions affect our dimension. In fact, if it weren't for the first seven dimensions we wouldn't be here. So why stop at seven? There could be other parallel dimensions that have special effects in our dimension. For instance, what are the attributes of any of the other dimensions? If I were to select the last dimension, the eleventh dimension, for no reason, can we prove this dimension does or does not affect the third dimension in some way? Therefore, is it possible the eleventh dimension has a force field that acts like a catalyst to promote chemical reactions that promotes DNA? I would not be surprised if Mr. Kaku would come up with mathematical proof of a parallel world that acts like a catalyst for life in our world, which I would gladly accept.

If this were true, what would be the signs of these catalytic reactions in our world? I would look for unrelated life forms in many parts of the world springing up under various conditions; from the real hot to the real cold. And this is exactly what we can find. It seems that life springs up like magic anywhere. We know this can't be magic, so there has to be a logical reason. Therefore, I propose some sort of catalystic force field from another dimension that promotes life here on Earth. If this is true, then life is not unique to Earth and there has to be life on other planets. Therefore, we should continue to send out those radio signals into space: "HELLO OUT THERE."

PART FOUR:

FUNDAMENTAL FORCES

Floating in Noise

CHAPTER 12

LIGHT

This chapter is not about phase change of metal, just the capability of metals/materials to glow during elevated temperatures, or, how electrons produce light when they fall to a lower shell in the molecule. At least, this was the idea until I realized that there could be other ways to make light. Therefore, I put together a list of ways that light could be generated.

The list is as follows.

1. Atomic energy:
    a. Sun
    b. Atomic Bomb
2. Potential difference:
    a. Lightning
    b. Small electrical discharges
3. Combustion (organic/inorganic):
    a. Solids
    b. Liquids
    c. Gas
4. Electricity:
    a. Incandescent
    b. Gas (elements)
    c. Laser

    d. L.E.D.
5. Chemical:
    a. Luminance (organic)
    b. Luminance (inorganic)
    c. Mixture (explosives)

I am sure that there are more ways that light is produced and could be added to this list, but as I looked this list over, I find only two ways that those molecules can make light and they are differentiated by being linear or omni light waves. Atomic energy, explosives and molten metals are where the electrons travel at high velocities in the outer orbits to make omni waves. L.E.D.s, lasers, and luminance are where the electrons drop back down into their stable shells, giving off signature RF frequencies of linear light.

As previously stated, light has two phases, linear directional and omni directional. The latter, omni directional, would be like dropping a pebble in water and seeing waves spread out in all directions from the impact. The linear directional wave would be like a wave traveling down a taut wire, as in string instruments.

A simple demonstration will show what a linear directional wave looks like and how polarization works with it. Procure a length of rope and two small slats (like rulers), then secure the rope at one end to a solid object and fix the slats one on each side of the rope vertically. We now give the rope a vertical shake. The wave will travel down the rope and will go by the vertical slats. But if we would put the slats horizontal and close to the rope, then shake the rope vertically again, the wave would be stopped at the slats. This is the general idea how polarized sunglasses work. We can stop part of the light that causes glare.

Noise

Note that as the electron is speeding around in its shell above the light barrier, a shock wave is formed (Wave Law #9) and that shock wave will produce multiple RF frequencies, or noise. Light is nothing but RF NOISE! That noise is only perceived as light when the photons/waves of the correct frequencies hit the rods and cones in our eyes. In the daytime, that noise is from the sun which permeates everything. If you would close your eyes you would see the world as it actually is, dark.

Omni Light Waves

Omni directional light is produced when metal (for example) is being heated to a high temperature. As it heats up, the metal will start to give off heat waves. With more heat energy, the metal will start to glow a soft orange light. Here, the electrons are not jumping shell levels, rather they are increasing their velocity around the outer shells to where they are in the shock wave velocity of fimenium (Wave Law #9). The hotter the metal becomes, the faster the electrons will move in the shock wave, and produce more wave frequencies, like 10-15HZ RF waves, or white light.

Linear Light Waves

Linear directional waves, or photons, are a more complicated to make. Note that heat (high energy) is not needed to make these waves, in fact, you could call it *cold light*, like in "Lightning Bug." We will start with one molecule in a normal state (room temperature).

All of the molecule's electrons are humming around in their designated rings or shells. Now we will allow a passing free electron in a higher state (higher velocity) to encounter our molecule and knock one of its electrons out of its present shell. With its higher velocity, this excited electron will be moved to a higher shell with higher potential energy. This is an unstable state as the electron is being coaxed back to its original shell by its protons. Being unstable, the electron will start to drop downward toward its original shell, but in doing so, will gain a higher velocity. This higher velocity will put the electron over the light barrier velocity and into the shock wave area (Wave Law #9). The shock wave will attenuate the higher velocity by turning it into a short burst of light-wave, in our case, a photon.

PHOTON

Reason tells me that a photon of light cannot be a wave and a particle at the same time. Light is a wave of the fifth-dimension medium. But if the packet of light is very small, I feel that it could react as a particle under certain circumstances. The linear light wave is asymmetric with an infinitely small width.

Emission Spectrum

All molecules have their own unique emission spectrum because of the different quantities of electrons changing shells in a molecule. When multi electrons go into the shock wave region, their velocities will vary, producing different RF wavelengths or in this case, bands of colors. Each electron may rebound several times, thus changing its speed/color before it settles down in its "comfortable" shell.

There are different materials available to produce linear directional waves of one color. This is found in L.E.D.s and crystals used in lasers.

Cherenkov Radiation

The Cherenkov Radiation is verification of what happens when a electron's velocity goes beyond the light barrier:

First: This is proof that electrons (in matter) can travel
faster than the speed of light, i.e., above the light
barrier velocity.

Second: This is validation that when an electron goes faster than
speed of light, it produces a shock wave, in this case,
R.F.Waves in the visible light spectrum
(which validates Wave Law #9).

This so called "Cherenkov Radiation" is really R.F. waves in the visible light range. The pictures of this phenomenon show that the light is blue. I believe that there was more than just the observed blue light, but the rest of the waves (as in noise) have been absorbed by the water medium used in the experiment.

Light Generation Drawings

At the end of this chapter are drawings 12.1 and 12.2 which pictorially show the electrons in their normal (A) state, then in their excited (B) state. Then, when they are in the excited state, the two methods (C & D) show how light is made. In "C," the electron falls back to its normal shell going through the shock wave, thus, velocity is given up for a photon. In "D," the excited electron is in a continuous velocity over the light barrier velocity, causing shock waves, or fimenium waves. You would find ultraviolet as the color of light from hydrogen in the plasma state.

Molecule Signature

Drawing 12.3 shows how a molecule in an excited state will give off its light signature when its' electron falls from the high energy shell down to its stable shell. To loose excess velocity, the electron (being attracted by the nucleus) will fall into the shock wave area and by friction (with fimenium), create a signature light wave. In this case, one can see how the electron will hunt, that is, bounce three times before settling down in its lower stable shell.

The Balmer emission spectrum for Protium (hydrogen) states that there are four lines of colors: red, blue, purple and purple. One can see why the last two colors will have the same energy levels.

Neutrons

The drawing 12.3 shows why the electron doesn't fall all the way into the nucleus to meet with the proton in its first fall. We are floating in fimenium, which means that all molecules are saturated with fimenium. That is no problem for protons as they are attracted to fimenium. But we know that the electron is also attracted to the proton, and at this moment, fimenium is overpowering and persuades the electron to go else where, like its own home shell. With the flooding of fimenium in all molecules, we can see the ease of making magnetism in any orbit or shell.

At absolute zero, with zero velocity, we now know why the electron in any molecule doesn't collapse into the nucleus and it is understandable why it takes high pressures or velocities to create neutrons due to the fimenium in the nucleus.

The word "SHELL" for the electrons' orbit now has a more solid meaning. We can see it is a fixed area, fixed by the protons' positive attraction and fimenium's negative repulsion for the electrons. With more protons and electrons in a molecule, the shells can get very complicated, but exacting.

CHAPTER 12

MOLECULE STATE

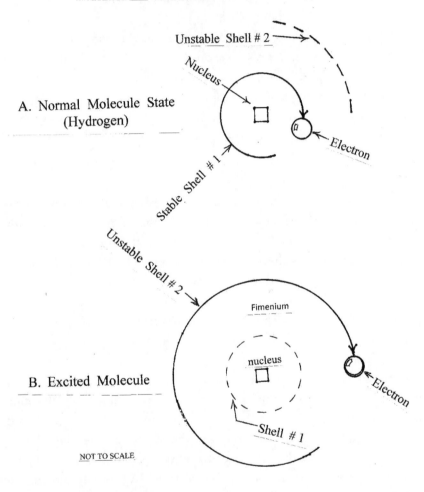

A. Normal Molecule State
(Hydrogen)

Unstable Shell # 2

Nucleus

Stable Shell # 1

Electron

B. Excited Molecule

Unstable Shell # 2

Fimenium

nucleus

Electron

Shell # 1

NOT TO SCALE

Drawing 12.1

LIGHT

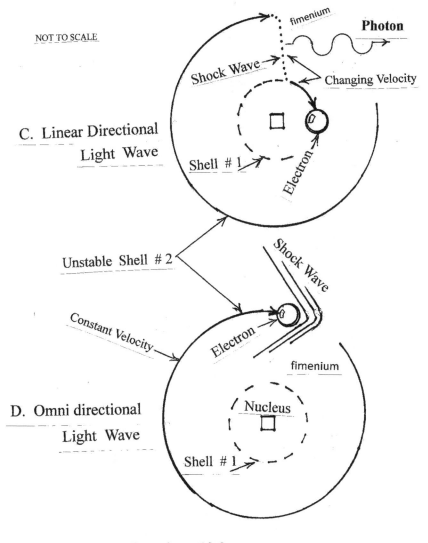

NOT TO SCALE

fimenium

Photon

Shock Wave

Changing Velocity

C. Linear Directional Light Wave

Shell # 1

Electron

Unstable Shell # 2

Shock Wave

Constant Velocity

Electron

fimenium

Nucleus

D. Omni directional Light Wave

Shell # 1

Drawing 12.2

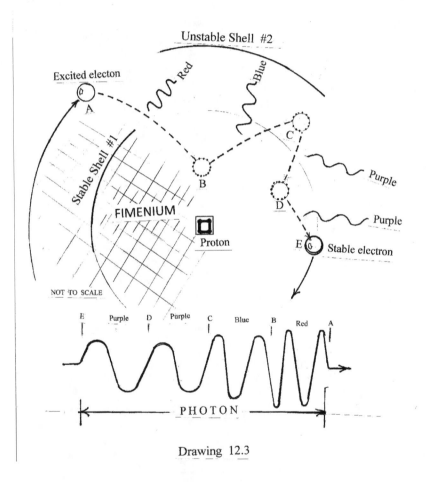

MOLECUE SIGNATURE
Hydrogen

Drawing 12.3

Beyond Light

CHAPTER 13
LIGHT TRAVEL

Up to 1945, we thought it was impossible to fly faster than the speed of sound --then a WWII fighter, the P47, tried to fly through the *sound barrier* ---- but instead, it almost got destroyed. That was farther proof that the sound barrier could not be breached. Several other methods were tried by brute force (bigger motors, bigger props) but the internal combustion engine and propeller system was not the way. It would take another type of engine.

In 1960 the X-1 rocket plane was dropped from a B-29 and flew through the sound barrier by brute force of a rocket engine. Today we have the French Concorde, which is a passenger plane that can fly beyond the sound barrier routinely. Now we have the X-43, which can fly over Mach 5.

What is the next barrier that we will break? Someday we will break the light barrier. It is a common occurrence for mother nature to break the light barrier, so it should be possible for us. What we need is the correct power system, which is beyond our present technology. But, I am confident that someday we will discover how the Warp Engine Drive in the Star Trek ship "Enterprise" works.

I believe that the Warp Engine will really be a fimenium engine. What I found interesting is that when I speculated on the fimenium engine, the space ship for that engine would look like a Flying Saucer! And I would expect the ship to glow from its engine or fuselage noise. This brings me much closer to believe in UFOs. I know it will be possible.

THE TRIP

If we had the Enterprise today, we could take a little trip. It would start out like this: we would leave the Earth's atmosphere at Mach 5 , then advance our speed. What we would notice would be the stars in front of us going more red and the stars behind us going more blue. This is nothing more than the Doppler effect (Wave Law #6). That is, the faster we go forward, we push the oncoming light waves together to create shorter wave length. The light waves behind us would be getting longer, or into the red range.

With our increase in speed, the light waves will get too short or long for us to see and the cosmos will become dark to us. No light, in front or the rear of our ship. In fact, we would not have light inside the ship, either! The fifth-dimension medium would be traveling through the ship at the same velocity as the ship is traveling. No third-dimension matter stops the fifth dimension-medium, as we know our flashlight will work in the deepest holes in the Earth or on any submarine. As we increase our velocity, the waves are becoming ever shorter, much beyond our visual range and into the dangerous range for humans.

Right now, this velocity would be dangerous for us as the fimenium would be speeding through the ship and us unless we had a negative shield, or the ship's outer shell charged negatively to deflect fimenium from going through the ship to around the ship. This is identical to an airplane: guiding the air around the aircraft. In both cases, we would be carrying our own supply of air or fimenium.

Eventually, we would reach the speed of light, and we would pass through it with maybe a slight shudder. Now beyond the light barrier, our ship is making a shock wave (see wave law #9). We know from the wave laws that the shock wave uses up energy, therefore, our velocity would be limited by our available power. The shock wave will contain a variety of fimenium waves, including all radio waves and light waves. In fact, our ship could be glowing with white light during this time. The higher our velocity, the shorter the waves will become until they become gamma-rays and X-rays, very dangerous to us so we would need good shielding. The shock wave will eventually absorb all the available energy of the ship's engine, limiting our velocity.

Side note: The shock wave is caused by all the electrons in the molecules on the front of our ship (like the bow on a boat). This would be the same shock wave of an electron going down a wire, but because of the size of our ship, the shock wave is much larger. We will need a negative shield around the ship to push fimenium aside.

CHAPTER 14
THE FUNDAMENTAL FORCES

The four fundamental forces as stated in Wikipedia dictionary are: *"Gravity, the Strong Force, the Weak Force and Magnetism."* I feel that is a misnomer as it should be: " *Static Electricity , Strong Force, Weak Force and Gravity"*. We know that it is the "Static Electrical Force" that keeps the electron in its orbit around a nucleus. The atom can survive without magnetism, but not without the static potential forces. The electron and proton have their own static fields which are opposite in polarity, i.e., positive and negative fields which form the cohesion forces to form the atom and which make magnetism possible.

We encounter the forces of gravity and static electricity as everyday experiences. We do not normally encounter the Strong and Weak Nuclear Forces as they are on the molecular level. Being such, there is a lot we don't know about these forces because they are really "fields," and as we now know, fields are of other dimensions. In this chapter, we will try to determine the origination of the Strong and Weak Nuclear Fields. The main fact that we know is that it is the Strong Nuclear Force Field that keeps the protons together in the nucleus, so we will focus our investigation on the Strong Force molecularly.

Magnetism

Magnetism will be the first force to be investigated. We know that there are repulsion forces between electrons, fimenium and the magnetic field when there is motion. But in static conditions, magnetism has no effect on the *polarity field* of the electron or proton, in other words, there is no interactions when a stationary magnetic field is next to a negative or positive field. Protons have an affinity for fimenium, not to magnetism as a separate entity. Note that this affinity is between each individual proton and fimenium, not between protons. Therefore, the affinity between protons and fimenium has no influence on the static repulsion force between protons. Because protons are oblivious to a magnetic field, the magnetic field is not the force that keeps protons together in the nucleus. I group magnetism along with compressed air: both easily made, both essential.

Static Electricity/Gravity

The next force we will look at is static electricity. Static electricity is really a misnomer because it is not electricity at rest, but rather a force field surrounding the electron and the proton. The repulsion force between two electrons or two protons is substantial, which means that it will take another force much greater to force two protons together in any nucleus.

Is gravity the force that can overcome the repulsion forces between protons? Then the question arises: " what particle in the third dimension does gravity work through or is gravity a part of every particle?" Previously, I believed that gravity was part of every electron and proton because that would be the only way that electrons and protons could attract each other in space to form hydrogen atoms. Then the hydrogen atoms would attract each other to form hydrogen stars.

If protons had gravitational attraction (along with their positive field), it has to be very weak as we do not find two protons together in any hydrogen molecules; it just does not happen. Therefore, to form deuterium and the heavier molecules, we are left with neutrons. Also, hydrogen can have two neutrons.

Neutron

Now we know what is keeping the protons in the nucleus together. From our investigations, it is not magnetism, static electricity or gravity. It all falls onto the neutron. But neutrons have lost their polarity forces and are in a neutral state. But how can this be? Why and how can a neutron being neutral keep two protons together as in helium? The only possibility that I can speculate on is that the neutron has dual personalities unlike nothing we have ever seen before.

Because the neutron is made up of an electron and a proton, we have to go back to the sixth and seventh-dimension origins to find any particularities responsible for the electron and proton particles. What secrets do the sixth and seventh-dimension have for us?

We are now in the Twilight Zone. I have found no physical proof to what happens to the fields of an electron and proton when they form a neutron. With reverse engineering, and the aid of the wave laws, it is possible to determine if a Strong Force and Weak Force could materialize from the union of an electron and a proton. I feel that those two force fields can be related, but even so, I have not been able to find any definitive information on the Weak Force; it's a vague force field.

Those who accept the String Theory should understand its relationship to the wave laws. Now, a short review of the String Theory for electrons and protons in their free state. The String Theory is all about particles being vibrating strings, which makes up particles like the protons and electrons as: "*wave like entities*". If this is true, then these particles should follow the wave laws, particularly wave law number 21, *heterodyning*. Because of contiguity, we can equate the polarity fields of the electron and proton to the same actual frequencies of their particles. We see the energy that those two dimensions have put into the electron and proton as polarity fields. What happens to the fields of the electrons and protons when those particles unite into a neutron?

When we apply the heterodyne law which states that when two different frequencies are superimposed, along with the two original frequencies, there will be two new frequencies: the sum and the difference. The sum should have twice the energy of the originals: making a new frequency/ force field, in this case, the "Strong Force." The difference in force field frequencies would be the smaller, or "Weak Force." The frequency of the two new force fields should be a higher and a lower frequency of the original frequencies; therefore, we may not detect them as polarity fields but as a different type of force field that we do not recognize due to the frequency change.

Thus, we can surmise that it is the Strong Force Field of the neutron that keeps the protons together in the nucleus, where other force fields could not. Being that it is the Strong Force Field which keeps the protons together, it would seem that the Strong Force Field would have used the negative component in the union of the electron and proton. This negative component would attract the protons but keep the electrons at a distance.

If the previous statement is true for the Strong Force, then the same rules should be true of the Weak Force. That is, the Weak Force should contain the positive component of the electron/proton union and being of lower frequency will have less energy but will be effective over a longer range. Do you see the implications of this scenario? The positive essence of the neutron has an attraction to all distant electrons! What we have now is that all molecules will be attracted to each other due to the attraction between all neutrons and all electrons. Gravity works in this manner.

I found it interesting that the Strong Force has a short effective range, whereas, the Weak Force has a long effective range. This implies that "strength times distance should equal *Fn.*" That is: strong force X distance = weak force X distance = *Fn*

Gravity

If I would hold a 2- pound pail of water 2 feet off the ground, I would feel the tug of gravity pulling the pail to the ground. I cannot detect any field between the pail and the ground. Because of the 2-foot height, the pail has 40 foot-pounds of potential energy, thus we have an *attraction force* between the pail and ground.

We cannot detect a field between the pail and the Earth to define a gravity field. Therefore, we have no proof/indication that gravity is from another dimension. I have not been able to detect any physical disturbances in our third dimension, like an unclaimed field, to indicate which parallel dimension gravity belongs to. All I can do is rely on our scholars who have studied gravity in great detail. Temporarily, I will go along with Mr. Albert Einstein, who said that gravity is from the fourth dimension.

I still have a problem in that my faith still lies with Mother Nature and her wave laws, especially law number 21: heterodyning. Heterodyning accounts for the strong force, therefore it should account for the weaker force which could be the force we know as gravity. Even though gravity is the weaker force, it makes up for it in its ability to attract over greater distances. The Weak Force is important for several reasons: it is allegedly responsible for the decay of a neutron and it is responsible for the forming of deuterium (gravity), which leads to fusion.

To summarize these findings: "Gravity is the attraction between two molecules," which is achieved by three forces:

1. The attraction force between the positive proton and the
negative electron.
This can form neutrons for:

2. The Strong Force which has a strong attraction
for protons over a short distance.

3. The Weak Force which has a weak attraction for all
electrons over a long distance.

Primary and Secondary Forces

We know that the two static force fields come from the sixth and seventh dimensions because of their disturbances in our third dimension. When those two potential forces come together we get two new forces: the Strong Nuclear Force and the Weak Nuclear Force. We can break these forces down into two groups.

I. Primary Forces
Positive Static Force
Negative Static Force

II. Secondary Forces
Strong Nuclear Force
Weak Nuclear Force: gravity.

The weak nuclear force needs more investigation. If the String Theory is correct, then gravity is a secondary force. If the String Theory is wrong, then gravity is a primary force from the fourth dimension as stated previously.

EPILOGUE

LIGHTNING
Oh, the beauty of lightning dancing in the night,
With power and majestic force, it gives off such light.

Helter skelter it dances across the sky,
As we hear the choirs of its thunderous cry.

Lightning up the skies in an uncertain path,
It races to meet the ground with its wrath.

Is it Mother Nature's torch to show off her creations,
Or, is it the Devil's spear for his damnations.

How its majestic powers can awe us,
And still, how lightning can scare us.

By JDC Nelson

Wave law #9 states that there is a shock wave beyond the barrier wave (terminal velocity of the medium). In Chapter one, lightning was discussed to show that a lightning strike went over the sound barrier and into the shock wave. The (sound) shock wave is recognizable by the "crack" it produces which is the same for the "crack" from a jet aircraft that has gone supersonic. That lightning "crack" has multiple sound frequencies in it. This is evident by the fact that the farther you are from the strike area, the lower the sound is, as the higher frequencies are attenuated faster.

Lightning has another side to it, too. We can detect lightning by the static that we can pick up on the radio. We know that it is the electrons as they flash through the sky that produce the static, but, just how is it done? We now know that the electrons have to go faster then the speed of light to produce a shock wave. The shock wave will have electrons moving at all velocities above the light barrier, which will give us unlimited radio frequency noises, our static: This is what shock waves do best.

Gamma Rays

Another example of velocities greater than the speed of light would be the quasars. We know that quasars produce gamma rays. What engine has enough energy to produce gamma rays? Gravity! A quasar will attract other celestial bodies at velocities much greater than the speed of light. Those bodies are moving at the velocity where their shock waves will produce gamma rays and X-rays. These high frequencies are what we pick up when we view quasars. I would expect that *black holes* would produce fimenium shock waves in those frequencies too.

Then there are the gamma-ray bursts that they are detecting from imploding stars. Here again, the star is collapsing faster than the speed of light, which will produce shock waves. These shock wave will produce much noise, in this case, gamma rays. It would be a short and powerful burst of high frequency waves.

Gravitational Lens / Dark Matter

We have seen that the proton has a strong affinity for the fifth-dimension medium. This would mean that there would be a heavy concentration of fimenium around and through any celestial body. Because gravity cannot bend light waves, this means that it is the dense fimenium field around a galaxy that bends the light waves around the star like a lens (wave law #23). There is a similar event when radio waves from a broadcasting station are transmitted, then part of the waves will bounce off the ionosphere and be reflected to distant parts of the world.

There is another interesting event that media can do, which happens in the ocean depths. It is not unusual to find layers of water at different temperatures at various depths. A layer of water with a different temperature from the adjoining layer will act like a channel and will guide sound waves within that channel.

Therefore, "Gravitational Lens" is a misnomer, and this effect should be known as "Fimenium Lensing" due to the attraction of fimenium around a planet causing a bending effect. Also, this atmosphere of fimenium, unseen, uncharted, untouchable mass is proof of what we call DARK MATTER. Fimenium may seem to be a weightless medium, but when you collect light years of it, the mass would be immense.

The test in which two atomic clocks were sent around the Earth in opposite directions and came back with a time shift is proof of a fimenium atmosphere around Earth. Because of the Earth rotating, the fimenium may not rotate at the same velocity as Earth. Fimenium would be a source of friction for any moving object in space. There is also the possibility of a fimenium space wind, which could affect just about anything.

Black Holes

There is a blue planet out in space that is named Earth.
The gravity is so strong that sound waves cannot leave it.
It is called "The Silent Planet."

There is a neutron planet out in space named Leavenworth.
The gravity is so strong that light waves cannot leave it.
It is called "The Black Hole."

J.D.C. Nelson

The reason for both of the above is the same, the captivity of the wave carrying medium by the planet. If light waves are unaffected by gravity, then how can we have Black Holes (wave law #20)?

There are two possibilities:

1. The Black Hole has ingested all of the fimenium around itself, leaving a fimenium void. No medium for light waves to travel and leave the Back Hole

2. The Black Hole has a very strong attraction for fimenium and so do the rest of the galaxies around the Black Hole. The struggle has made the fimenium around the Black Hole so stretched or sparse that the fimenium field cannot carry a wave as we know it. This would be like our mesosphere where the air is too thin to carry sound waves.

Inside the atmosphere of the Black Hole, it should be active with fimenium waves from the energy it has collected from other planets via space rock. Just like our world, our atmosphere is very active with noise from lightning and meteors but none of that noise escapes into the void.

Big Bang Theory.

Our cosmos started at one point in space with a tremendous explosion with an small amount of dense matter. I used to believe that, but this book changed my mind. This author has convinced me that it wasn't as simple as "one Big Bang."

I know of five different dimensions, but I have heard that there are at least 11 dimensions. Of the dimensions that I know of, each is a singularity with our third dimension having the desolated stage. It is important to know that our domain was completely empty at the beginning of time. Then it is said that the Big Bang brought everything into our third dimension in a split second. Mother Nature had a rift go through all 11 dimensions at the same instant, same area? I think that she was smarter than that.

If everything came through the rift at the same time with an explosion at the speed of light, all of the material would still be going away from that EVENT at the speed of light. The third dimension was completely empty; there was nothing to cause friction. All of the fimenium would have attached itself to protons and would still be expanding into the cosmos at the speed of light.

The fifth dimension had to come through the rift first and fill up the third dimension with fimenium. Now, when the protons (electrons later) came through the rift into the third dimension, probably traveling faster than the speed of light, friction due to fimenium would have caused these new particles to slow down to the present state. At those velocities, micro waves and other fimenium waves would have filled the cosmos. Fimenium means friction to everything moving in the third dimension. This would include anything in orbit along with the space rockets.

FINIS

It is really odd that how much we depend on waves as our main communication means, our source of light and heat, yet there is no such commodity as waves. Energy and time fall in the same category, for instance:

WAVES: the progressively transferring of energy
between particles.

ENERGY: the relative motion between two particles.

TIME: the elapse of movement between two particles
in a chronological order.

It is interesting to note that before the Big Bang
on the empty stage of the third dimension ,
THERE WERE NO WAVES,
NO ENERGY, AND
NO TIME.

THANK YOU

I want to acknowledge that my discoveries on waves would not have been possible without Mr. Michio Kakus' book "PARALLEL WORLDS," which opened the fifth dimension to me as light waves. Thank you much, Professor Kaku.

I also need to thank Mr. Brian Greene for his book "THE FABRIC OF THE COSMOS," which opened the door for the sixth dimension for me.

A big thank you goes to my wife, Lucy, who had to put up with my endless talk on physics which always left her baffled. She never understood my great interest in physics but was always patient and never threw anything at me, but I am sure she would of liked to.

I want to thank my brother Bill (Willy) for listening to and patronizing me when I talk about the material in this book when he did not understand a single word that I spoke. It was a tough job, but it helped me to think things through. We need to thank Bill for serving our country as an Army GI Joe.

And I want to thank my cousin Floyd Bourbon (Butch) for his time in reviewing my work and discussing some of the problems. He is a retired Marine and Navy man so we want to thank him for serving our country for 20-plus years.

And last, but not least, I want to thank Bill Hammond for proof reading my manuscript. Bill did an excellent job in finding my numerous errors. I really believe that Bill could spot a misplaced period from 50 paces off. Bill is the Features Copydesk Chief at the Minneapolis Star Tribune, and he is also an ex Navy man whom we owe our thanks for serving our country.

Jerry